THE BUSINESS OF

NONPROFIT

YOUR SUCCESS

IS MY BUSINESS

TEMPLE B. RAGLAND, JR.

Penny Steele, Editor

The Business of Nonprofit
Copyright © 2018 by Temple B. Ragland, Jr
Direction New Publishing Company

About the Author

Temple Bates Ragland, Jr. is a business consultant with over 45 years experience and successes in the business world. His knowledge and expertise has been praised by boards, executive directors, investors and grantors all across the United States, and Kenya, and Nigeria, Africa. Ragland was educated in Chattanooga, Tennessee and Ohio University, Athens, Ohio where he was a member of Sigma Delta Chi, the Society of Professional Journalists. This man of Kappa Alpha Psi lives in Chattanooga, Tennessee.

Table of Contents

1

HURRICANE MATTHEW

Hurricane Matthew had just left the low country of South Carolina. The land was devastated. Residents of the area were disheartened, depressed, and devastated. There had been no water or electricity for three whole days. Some residents had to go as far away as Tennessee to be able to live. Roberta and Pooky looked at the torn land in disbelief.

Roberta asked, "What can be done? What can de done?"

"I wish that there was something that could be done," answered Pooky.

They both talked about their conversation of last week. They wanted to be able to change or improve the lives of the residents, friends, family, neighbors, and, especially, the children in Yemassee, Sheldon, and all the low lying areas of the low country of South Carolina.

Just the week before, Roberta and Pooky were talking about looking into, maybe, forming a nonprofit corporation. But neither knew a thing about a nonprofit corporation, a nonprofit organization, or just how this worked.

Roberta said that she had done a little research. From what she could figure out, a nonprofit organization is an organization *whose purpose is something other than making a profit.* Pooky was confused at this explanation and said so. She understood profit. Nonprofit didn't make good sense to her, and she said so.

Last week Roberta and Pooky had been talking about what they could do to make youth in the community happier. A great number of the kids in the community had to travel long distances to school. When they finally got home in the afternoons and on the weekends, they really had nothing to do. They had nothing to do that was fun or made them happy.

Roberta said that she had "asked around" about forming an organization that would help. She'd even tried to Google. The best understanding that she had come up with was that *a nonprofit corporation or organization provided programs and services. These programs and services helped others to have a better life.* She figured that she and Pooky could do that, if they just clearly understood.

"The first thing you need to form a nonprofit corporation or organization," Roberta said "is a charter, *or articles of incorporation.* We'd get that from the South Carolina Secretary of State. In all fifty states, you get a charter from your Secretary of State."

"This charter asks for very simple information. You'll need the name and address of your organization. You'll need one person to serve as *the registered agent.* You'll need a purpose, usually three incorporators; and you'll need to answer two to three other very simple questions."

"You can actually do this online. However, you can also mail the charter back to your Secretary of State. Each state has its own price for a charter. The fee is usually $100.00 payable to the Secretary of State.

Twenty-four hours later, Pooky was on the phone talking to Roberta. "You were right, Ro." Pooky explained that she had gone online to the South Carolina Secretary of State and found how easy it was to apply for a charter.

"All that's needed for us to get a charter is to go online and download the application. I'm excited! We need to choose a name for out nonprofit today!"

"On the application we need the name of our nonprofit, our address, and the name of our registered agent. A registered agent is the person that will be responsible for receiving any form of communication from the Secretary of State."

"The only communication that is received is a reminder that once a year our nonprofit has to renew our charter. The notice comes in January in most states, and you have ninety days to pay the ten or twenty dollars. This fee depends on in what state you reside."

"We also have to define what kind of nonprofit we are. We have the choice to be a public benefit or religious nonprofit."

"We need a dissolution clause that tells what we'll do if we dissolve our nonprofit. The form already has this printed. We just have to check a space."

'We need three incorporators. An incorporator is just a witness, or anyone, who is in favor of our nonprofit. There is no requirement on age or where the incorporator resides. They can live in Atlanta or Indianapolis, Indiana. Each incorporator has to sign the Articles of Incorporation Application."

"The cost to file the application is only $25.00 in South Carolina. I couldn't believe it. It's only $25.00! In Georgia and Tennessee it's $100.00."

From her research, Roberta knew that the nonprofit would need an EIN. An EIN is an Employer Identification Number. Whether you have employees or not, a nonprofit needs an EIN. The IRS requires all businesses to have an EIN.

You can easily get an EIN online. And the EIN number is free. *Make certain that you go to **irs.gov**.* Other sites will usually charge you to do what you can do for free. To get an EIN takes all of 300 seconds, if that long. It's valid and operative as soon as you get it online.

Pooky wanted to know if they could begin to help people when they get their charter and EIN.

"We'll be a nonprofit when we get the charter and EIN, but we'll need money for the programs and services that we decide on," Roberta said. "In order to get money for the things that we need to provide the programs and services, we'll need to be a 501(c)(3) *tax exempt nonprofit corporation.*

2

TAX EXEMPT STATUS

"Tax exempt. What in the world does that mean? Let me guess," Pooky said. "We won't have to pay any taxes, right?"

Roberta slowly smiled. She told Pooky that a great majority of folks say and believe this when they hear the words tax exempt. She explained that to think that is wrong. Roberta said, "That is not what tax exempt means. Tax exempt is an IRS definition that means that a person can give you money or a gift, *and they can take a tax deduction.* A foundation or a business can give you grant money, and they can take a tax deduction."

"For instance," Roberta continued, "Suppose that we had a group of middle school kids, and one of our programs for the year would be to transport them to events and activities once a month. We might want to take them fishing one month, and down to SCAD (Savannah College of Art and Design) during another month. We would need transportation."

" We could approach one of the automobile dealerships here and see if they'd donate a van. It could be a used or new van. They would, at least, give the idea consideration, because, if nothing else, the dealership could take a tax deduction. It benefits them and us."

"All businesses like to take tax deduction," Roberta said. "I've heard that Panera Bread and Publix in the low country will donate bakery products to any kind of tax exempt nonprofit programs. Just think about childcare centers and senior daycare food programs that need bread and any kind of free bakery products." Roberta exclaimed.

Pooky chimed in, "Not only will this be a big help for those in need at Thanksgiving and Christmas, but every week!"

"You're so right," Roberta answered. "All that's needed is for us to take a 501(c)(3) exemption letter to Panera and Publix. They'd be happy to donate and take a tax deduction."

In Roberta's research, she'd discovered that the vast majority of federal programs which provide money to childcare centers, assisted and supportive living facilities, neighborhood development initiatives, art programs, or any other programs requesting grant money, now require tax exempt status. You need a 501(c)(3).

A few years ago, a nonprofit corporation or organization didn't always need tax exempt status to receive grant money, in kind services, or technical help from the U.S. Departments of Housing and Urban Development, Health and Human Services, Education, or Justice. Now, in 95% of all cases, you do need tax exempt status.

"Do you now understand the importance of tax exempt status in what we want to do?" Roberta asked Pooky.

11

3

BYLAWS

Pooky and Roberta were standing in front of The Coffin Point Praise House on St. Helena Island, South Carolina. Praise houses got their name from what the Gullah inhabitants of the low country called "prays house."

Built by slaves as a place for prayer, praise houses were very small frame structures, usually, 10 feet by 14 or 15 feet. Slave owners made certain that they were small, as they feared that too many slaves meeting together would cause major problems.

Praise houses were, also, used for other kinds of "gatherings." Music and singing were a big part of praise house meetings. Slaves used them as a kind of courthouse to handle their own disputes. There were *laws by which* they did things in the praise house, especially, when it came to settling slave matters.

"Getting tax exempt status would help us," Pooky said.

Roberta could tell that Pooky was really interested in starting a nonprofit organization. When she told her that the second step and requirement in getting tax exempt status was to have bylaws, the first thing out of Pooky's mouth was "What are bylaws?

"Bylaws are the laws needed to operate our nonprofit," Roberta explained. "They are the *laws by which* a real organization is run."

"They are our road map. They are the rules and laws that we establish to manage and regulate our nonprofit. When we have our rules and laws down on paper, it'll dictate how we handle any situations or issues which might come up."

"I know that it'll help us stay away from conflicts of interest. Besides that, the IRS requires that we have bylaws if we're going to apply for tax exempt status."

Deep in thought, Pooky remembered her folks telling her about the praise house. Her folks, like Roberta's people, were born in the low country. They were born there and had never left. They weren't "come heres," as those who were born in the low country called the people who moved to the low country from somewhere else. Pooky's and Roberta's folks were truly from the low country.

"Coffin Point Praise House is still standing for a reason. It was just waiting for us to sit down in front of it and make our bylaws. It's fitting. It survived the fire. It survived Matthew. Let's come back here and come up with some bylaws," Pooky said breaking her silence.

Two days later, Roberta and Pooky were back at Coffin Point sitting in front of the praise house. Both were excited. Both had researched and asked others about what to include in their bylaws and if there was anything that you had to have. Roberta had even looked at her church's bylaws. Pooky had fournd an example of bylaws on the Internet.

Both, Pooky and Roberta, were certain that no one could tell you what was needed in another organization's bylaws, or what rules or policies you had to have. You could have anything in your bylaws that you wanted.

Pooky had read and pretty much figured that they'd *certainly need articles* that covered the following specific information:

1. The name of their organization.
2. The address.
3. The purpose of the organization.
4. The names of their boards of directors and their addresses.
5. The titles of their directors.
6. The duties of their directors.
7. When and where meetings of the board would be held.
8. How board members would be elected; how often they would be elected; and how they would be removed, if necessary.
9. A conflict of interest policy.
10. Identification of committees.
11. Their financial policies.
12. A miscellaneous article.

4

NONPROFIT BUSINESS PLAN

"Pooky, I've been thinking." Roberta was in a pensive mood. They were in an area where the Yamasee Native American tribe had lived during the 1700's. It's where their hometown, Yamassee, South Carolina, had gotten its name.

The hot subtropical climate of the low country was considered perfect for rice and indigo growing. Slave owners depended upon the expertise of especially selected slaves who had learned how to grow rice or indigo in Africa.

These slaves were used to develop profitable plantations with booming rice and indigo businesses creating great wealth for slave owners. Both Roberta's and Pooky's families were descendants of the original slaves who were brought to the area and later made it their home.

"We're going to need a business plan." Roberta thought out loud.

Pooky was puzzled. "A business plan for our nonprofit?" she asked. "I didn't know that we were getting ready to start a business."

Roberta made it clear that both money making for profit and nonprofit corporations were businesses.

"If we're going to really make a difference, if we're going to succeed, we're going to operate like a business. All businesses need a business plan, Pooky."

They began brainstorming and came up with an approach to a business plan. They decided that they needed to decide *what* they were going to do; *why* they were going to do it; *who* they were going to create programs for; *where* they were going to do whatever they chose to do; *when* they were going to do this; and *how* they were going to accomplish their plans.

Three days later they had the layout for their business plan. Roberta's friend had delivered! It turns out that her friend is an expert in nonprofit matters, including business plans. After carefully discussing what had been offered, Pooky and Roberta decided to go with the friend's professional approach and outline. The following is the information they received:

Why Is A Business Plan Needed?

There are a couple of major reasons.

1. A business plan serves as a guide and a map to ensure success.

2. A business plan represents the nonprofit when no one is *physically* present to represent the nonprofit. An example of this is the investor or funder who might ask for your nonprofit's business plan.

17

Divide your business plan into six sections. These sections will answer each *who, what, when, where, why, and how question.*

The sections are Strategy Issues, Marketing Issues, Service Issues, Product Issues, Financial Issues, and SWOT Analysis (**Strengths, Weaknesses, Opportunities, and Threats** Analysis). Use the following format:

Section I: Strategy Issues

1. Identity. Define what *legal status* you want for your nonprofit. You have choices. You can be a simple tax exempt nonprofit corporation, or you can be a tax exempt nonprofit umbrella corporation. With the umbrella corporation, you can take advantage of a **dba designation.**

2. Purpose or Mission. This gives you a chance to determine what exactly your purpose for the nonprofit is. You can state what your mission and your goals are.

3. Management Team. You'll decide who or what make the final decisions for the nonprofit. Your Executive Board of Directors usually makes the final decisions. It's a great idea to have board members provide a brief resume.

4. I. T. How are you going to utilize information technology for the benefit or success of your organization?

18

Section II: Marketing Issues

The most important part of your business plan is your marketing plan. Your nonprofit corporation is a business. Every business needs a marketing plan. Marketing is the foundation of every successful business.

Marketing is not advertising, promotion, or public relations. Advertising, promotion, and public relations are *marketing tools*, which are used to successfully accomplish your marketing plan.

Marketing is simply figuring out who or what you are trying to reach and how to reach them. Marketing is determining your market and how you will successfully connect with that market.

You will make use of the M.A.P. (Marketing Action Plan) Format. The M.A.P. defines your nonprofit's *goals, objectives,* and *action plans.* Your *action plans* describe step-by-step how you will accomplish your *goals* and *objectives.*

1. <u>M.A.P. (Marketing Action Plan)</u>. Your Marketing Action Plan (M.A.P.) will be divided into three (3) parts. They are:

    <u>Goals</u>. Your goals state what you plan to do.

    <u>Objectives</u>. Your objectives concentrate on *numbers*. Your number might be a date. Your number might be a number of people. The number could be a percentage of people. Your number might be an amount of money. For your purposes, your objective will *always have a number, or combination of* numbers.

19

Action Plan. Your action plan gives a specific and detailed description of how your nonprofit is going to accomplish your goals and objectives.

2. The M.A.P. Format:

Marketing Issue 1
- Goal 1
- Objective 1
- Action Plan 1

Marketing Issue 2
- Goal 1
- Objective 1
- Action Plan 1

3. Two Very Simple "Examples" of the M.A.P. Format:

Step One in Establishing Our Nonprofit

- Goal 1: To obtain articles of incorporation (charter) from The Secretary of State.

- Objective 1: To have obtained the charter by a specific DATE.

- Action Plan 1: We will apply online with the following required information: the name of our nonprofit, address, purpose, registered agent, whether we are a public or religious organization, the name of our incorporators, what county and country we are in. We will pay the filing fee online.

Step Two in Establishing Our Nonprofit

- Goal 2: To get an EIN (Employer Identification Number).

- Objective 2: We will apply for the EIN 30 minutes after we receive our charter.

- Action Plan 2: We will go online to IRS.Gov and supply the required information. We will have this no later than five (5) minutes after we apply. The EIN is valid and operational as soon as it is issued online. The EIN is free from the IRS.

"Hey, this M.A.P. information is good stuff. It's simple if you just follow this outline," Pooky said.

"Yes, those examples are very helpful. We're going to have to be very, very specific in all of our goals, objectives, and action plans," Roberta answered.

She knew that they were going to have quite a few goals, objectives, and action plans. They would have goals, objectives, and action plans for the nonprofit; and for each program and service they would have goals, objectives, and action plans.

"Pooky, we're really going to be ready when we finish our M.A.P.," Roberta said.

Section III: What Are You "Selling?"

You might think that your nonprofit does not sell anything. It has no products. It has no merchandise. McDonalds has products and merchandise.

But that's not what Mickey D sells. They don't sell hamburgers or "fries to go with that shake." All of the fast food places sell burgers and fries. You can get a burger at Taco Bell. It's just in a different bun!

McDonald's is selling the *exact* same thing that your nonprofit will be selling. They sell *benefits*. **Your nonprofit will be selling benefits.**

There are two kinds of benefits. There are fiscal benefits. There are emotional benefits.

1. Fiscal Benefit.

What is a Fiscal Benefit? A fiscal benefit is any benefit that will make a pocketbook or bank account smile. Picture the amount of money that you can save a person or an organization if your nonprofit organization is tax exempt. The grantor can give you money and take a tax deduction. Your organization then has funds to provide programs and services.

Fiscal Benefits Get Funding. When you present a proposal that assures a grantor that your program or project is fiscally beneficial to them, you have been

22

successful. You have sold a fiscal benefit. Always remember that programs that are beneficial are the successful programs.

2. Emotional Benefit.

What is an Emotional Benefit? An emotional benefit is a benefit that makes *you* smile, makes you feel good inside, makes you happy.

Making a Mother and Child Happy. Picture the mother who has a child who is larger than other kids. She's unable to find a children's store or children's department, which carries her child's sizes. She feels terrible having to take her child to shop in adult stores. Unlike most kids, her child hates going to the mall, because they have to shop in adult stores.

Now a children's store opens that carries sizes for larger kids. In this new store, mom finds exactly what she wants for her child. She's happy because her child is now happy. When shopping, her child will never have to feel "out of place" again. She will buy forever at this store for her child.

The new children's store has gained her loyalty, because they have provided her an emotional benefit. They've made her happy. They've made her child happy.

Cooking Thanksgiving Dinner. The Thanksgiving holiday is in a couple of weeks. This year the family cook won't have to call in-laws, friends, or family members to know how to cook that turkey.

The cook has spent the past two years cooking his turkey with recipes from New England, N'awlins, and other cooking show recipes. Not this year. When the family watches Alabama or Michigan play football this Thanksgiving weekend, they will be eating bird and fixin's that the cook made from scratch from his own recipes!

What a feeling of accomplishment...made the cook feel *good all over.*

You now have to decide what benefits your nonprofit is going to offer that makes it attractive and creates an image that will draw funders. What fiscal and emotional benefits will your nonprofit feature?

Section IV: Product Issues

Imagine this. You're being interviewed on a television talk show. Why? Your nonprofit has been wildly successful.

It's a brand new experience, being in front of the bright lights and having a makeup artist work on you. It doesn't concern you at all. You're confident. You're ready.

You're ready for any kind of question or questions. The interviewer asks you to explain your "product" to the viewers.

"What is your model? What map or strategic plan did you follow that made your nonprofit so successful?" The talk show interviewer asks.

You don't even have to think. You explain:

24

1. The First Step: "The very first step in developing *any* successful business model is to create a business plan."

   "This was the very first thing I did. I recognized that a nonprofit corporation is a business. Our nonprofit's business plan was the first component of my product or model for success."

2. The Second Step: "My second step was to make sure that people immediately, and forever, recognized our nonprofit," you continued, "by choosing a unique name, symbol, template, or feature to describe it. Choose one or a combination of these distinctive features:"

   The Swoosh: You pointed out that, "When you see the swoosh symbol, you immediately know what tennis shoe comes to your mind."

   The Red and White Can: "A red and white can is something that makes you real thirsty for a specific soda."

   The Red Cross: "A huge red cross on the side of a building brings to mind the nonprofit that helps with disaster."

   Arms and Legs Flaying: "You know you can "cool off " when you see that clear container, arms and legs flaying in the air and liquid sloshing about."

"You need some feature that will set your nonprofit *apart* from other nonprofits, and single you out as not just a *part of* the usual nonprofit crowd."

3. The Third Step: "The third part of my product (model) is innovation and creativity."

"You want exciting, meaningful, and beneficial programs and services that are going to improve the lives and circumstances of those you're going to help. Make your programs and services interesting as well as helpful."

Kids and Computers: "Consider mentoring. A lot of nonprofits offer mentoring and training. Instead of the usual computer training for kids, make using computers exciting and interesting."

"How?" you ask."

"Kids already know much, much more about computers than their mentors. Have weekend classes where kids can teach adults! Kids will jump at the chance to be able to "tell their parents' and other adults what to do."

"This is the "different approach, which will set you apart from the usual "mentor computer" programs.

Veterans Newspaper: "Take another fresh approach to programs and services to attract those you're trying to help and also attract funders."

"Your nonprofit might operate an assisted and s upportive living facility. You might have veterans l iving there."

"Let the veterans create and publish a newspaper and mail it to other assisted and supportive living facilities in the region where veterans live. It will add enjoyment and excitement for your veterans. Again, make your approach innovative."

As you leave the television studio, you go over your interview in your mind. You described your specific product. You explained what made your nonprofit successful. You know that if others use your approach, or something akin to it, of developing a business plan, creating a brand identity, and establishing innovative and exciting programs and services; they will be successful, too. It's been a good day.

Section V: Financial Issues (The Budget)

The very first thing that people worry about or try to finish is the budget. This is exactly the wrong approach to take. When creating a budget, always remember that programs and services determine your budget. Read that last line again.

1. <u>Programs and Services Determine Your Budget</u>.

You will never know what funds are needed if you haven't determined what you are going to do. You won't know what money you need if you haven't finalized the programs and services you will offer.

After you decide upon your programs and service, only then can you sensibly create your *line item budget*.

2. <u>Never Guesstimate or Speculate</u>. You should never guesstimate or speculate how much money you will need to operate your programs and services.

3. <u>Create A Line Item Budget</u>. You want to create a *line item budget*. A line item budget is a budget where each expense is listed separately. Each line item has its own specific dollar amount. Guessing the amount is a bad practice!

4. <u>Annual Line Item Budget "SAMPLE"</u>. See below for a sample budget covering one year.

"SAMPLE"
Yearly Line Item Budget

- Personnel..
- Fringe Benefits (Multiply .20 x Personnel)..................
- Occupancy (Rent/Mortgage/Lease to Buy)...........
- Utilities
    o Electricity.....................................
    o Water...
    o Land Line.....................................
- Office Equipment.....................................
- Office Supplies..
- Program Supplies......................................
- Program Equipment...................................
- Insurance...
- Licenses, Permits, Certifications.......................

- Security...
- Marketing...
- Printing...
- Postage...
- Transportation......................................
- Travel...
- Consultants...
- Conferences...

Section VI: SWOT Analysis

SO, now you have a business plan structure. You feel like you're ready to move forward...ready to roll!

It's important that you take the next major step now. You could have taken this step before you even began your business plan. There's nothing wrong with that. However, if you haven't already done this step, you need to make certain that immediately after you finish the first five sections of your business plan; you perform a SWOT analysis.

SWOT stands for strengths, weaknesses, opportunities, and threats. Once you complete this you'll know if your nonprofit will work to improve what you want to improve or change what you're seeking to change.

1. Strengths. Begin by listing what you feel are your strengths.

Programs and Services. Do you have the programs and services that suit and match what you're trying to accomplish?

Staff. Do you have enough staff, including volunteers and collaborative partners, to accomplish your goals?

Partnerships. Are you committed to building collaborative partnerships?

Reputation. Will your nonprofit have the reputation as the organization that "gets things done? Your reputation is one of your strongest assets.

2. Weaknesses.

Lack. When there is a need for resources or personnel, this may be considered a weakness. Lack of clarity within an organization can be a weakness.

Conflict. When there is internal disagreement or conflict, this may result in weakness.

Examples of weaknesses include:

- Lack of staff.
- No written program procedures.
- Lack of staff & volunteer training.
- Lack of facilities.
- Lack of funding
- Disagreements among personnel0

3. Opportunities.

Community Involvement. Take the opportunity to become a real and beneficial member of the community where your programs are going to exist.

Demographics. Take advantage of demographic knowledge. Know the makeup of your recipients.

Go online to census.gov and enter your zip code. You'll get all of the demographic information that you'll ever need.

After you get this information, go to your local regional planning agency or local chamber of commerce and get their demographic information.
Funding Sources. Search and find funding sources.
Grants are a tremendous source of funds. Both government and foundation grants are available to help you successfully operate your program.

Remember…grants are not announced in order to refuse the applicants. Grants are there to help nonprofits operate beneficial programs and services.

Funders love deductions. Take the opportunity to help a foundation take a tax deduction!

Collaborative Partnerships. Take every opportunity to form collaborative partnerships, especially when just beginning your nonprofit. Look to partner with:

- Academia.
- The Business Community.
- Government Entities.
- Other Community Groups & Nonprofits.

Develop strong collaborative relationships. Your partner might give you nonprofit space or other resources to help operate your startup programs and services.

Do not be afraid to form these partnerships. Nobody is going to steal "your program." Do not have this mindset, PLEASE.

You cannot do everything that you want to do by yourself. You want others to duplicate what you're doing, because your programs and services help.

4. Threats. The greatest threats are those within yourself or your personnel. Among others these include:

Complacency

Laziness

Fear

Thinking Small

Refusal to Collaborate

Unwillingness to Consider New Ideas

5

APPLYING FOR YOUR 501(C)(3)

Roberta and Pooky had invited 'their expert' over to the heart of the low country to help them decide on the best approach for them to take in order to get their 501(c) (3) tax-exempt status. This Gullah Thanksgiving would be one which their guest would always remember. They had promised to take him fishing and introduce him to some real home cooked Gullah foods.

The three of them were walking along the winding roads of Fripp Island, one of Pooky and Roberta's favorite low country spots. Although late November, the temperature was usual, for this time of year, seventy degrees. Moss hanging from the big oak trees gave their guest an eerie kind of feeling. He said he'd never seen anything so striking.

"Wait until you see all of the low country around here," Roberta commented. "You ain't seen nothing yet."

"Roberta, you know we have a guest. You know that you meant to say "You haven't seen anything yet."" Pooky said grinning.

The friends doubled over in laughter. Then they got serious.

"We want to get a 501(c)(3). What do we need to do?" Pooky asked their expert.

As they stood there among the big oaks, their expert began to tell them how to get their tax-exempt status. He knew that they had their Articles of Incorporation, their EIN, and had pretty much settled on their nonprofit's bylaws. These are all needed to file the 1023 application with the IRS requesting status as a 501(c)(3).

"You need to get a 1023 Application from the IRS," he began.

"You can download the standard 26 page form, complete it, and mail it in to Covington, Kentucky. The address is:"

Internal Revenue Service
P.O. Box 12192
Covington, KY 41012-0192.

"Or you can apply for a 501(c)(3) online. The important thing to remember is this:"

"If you feel that your whole gross receipts will not exceed ten thousand dollars ($10,000.00) a year, the fee for your 501(c)(3) is two hundred and seventy-five dollars ($275.00)."

"If your gross receipts are going to exceed ten thousand dollars ($10,000.00) yearly, the fee is eight hundred dollars ($800.00)."

"It's up to you to decide this. You make this decision."

"When you download your 1023 application, don't let it scare you," he advised them. "The application has twenty-six pages, but all of the pages don't pertain to your nonprofit. To complete certain pages you might need some legal knowledge or basic accounting knowledge."

Their expert suggested that, if need be seek the help of someone who has *experience* in filing 1023 applications. Do not look for just any attorney or any accountant. It is essential to find someone who has experience in filing 1023 applications.

"I am going to ease your fears regarding the length of the application and its seemingly complicated parts. You will see the exact same parts to the application that I'm about to break down for you."

"The advice that I provide will make you smile and realize that filing is not going to be hard. You already have some of the information. Your completed business plan will provide you with much of the information that you need. It's not going to be as difficult as it first appears."

Roberta and Pooky were thrilled when their expert advised them in detail how to complete each section of the 1023 Application as follows:

Part I: Identification of Applicant.

Lines 1 - 4: Provide your nonprofit's name, address, and EIN.

Line 5: Fill in the month that will end your accounting period.

Line 6: Complete with your contact person's name, phone and fax (if there is one).

Line 7: Check "No" unless you plan to have an authorized representative, such as an attorney or accountant, handle all your communications with the IRS. Then additional forms must be completed.

Line 8: State whether you have had a person other than one of your board of directors, officers, trustees, or an authorized representative help you prepare your application. Check "Yes" if you paid someone to prepare your 1023 Application. Otherwise, check "No."

Line 9: Provide your nonprofit's website and email.

Line 10: Check "No" in response to the question. Your nonprofit *will* have to file a Form 990.

Line 11: Fill in with the date of incorporation on your papers of incorporation.

Line 12: Check "No" when you were formed under the laws of the United States.

Part II: Organizational Structure.

Lines 1 & 5: Check "Yes" since you already have incorporated and have written bylaws.

Lines 2, 3, 4a & 4b: Check "No."

Part III: Required Provisions in Your Organizing Document.

Line 1: Check the box and fill in the blank line as follows: Exempt Purpose Clause Amendment to Articles of Incorporation

Line 2a: Check the box since you do have a Dissolution Clause Amendment to your Articles of Incorporation.

Line 2b: Fill in the blank with "Dissolution Clause Amendment to Articles of Incorporation."

Line 2c: Skip this line and leave the box blank.

Part IV: Narrative Description of Your Activities.

This is where your completed Business Plan is certainly going to help you. Since your nonprofit is brand new, describe *your planned activities.* In your narrative describe in detail:

- What your planned activities are.
- Why you're going to provide them.
- Who you will provide them for.
- Where you'll provide them.
- When you'll provide them.
- How you plan to implement your activities.

It's important that your description is "thorough and accurate" as "it will be open for public inspection."

Part V: Compensation and Other Financial Arrangements With Your Officers, Directors, Trustees, Employees, and Independent Contractors.

Line 1a: Fill-in the name, title, and mailing address for each individual who will be serving as an officer, director, or trustee for your nonprofit. For everyone put **none** for compensation. *Your nonprofit will not pay compensation to any officers, members of your board of directors, or trustees.*

Line 1b: Write **none**.

Lines 2a through 9f: Check the correct yes or no answer and provide supporting documentation, if requested. When you are not certain how to answer any question or to prepare supporting documentation, be sure to consult with an individual who has experience and expertise in completing the 1023 Application. Do not be shy or hesitant. Ask to be certain.

Part VI: Your Members and Other Individuals and Organizations That Receive Benefits From You

Line 1a: If your nonprofit plans to serve **individuals** with goods, services, or funds, check "Yes." Then attach a description of each of your planned programs. Otherwise, check "No."

Line 1b: If your nonprofit plans to serve **organizations** with goods, services, or funds, check "Yes." Then attach a description of each of your planned programs. Otherwise check "No."

Line 2: You should check "No." As a 501 (c) (3) nonprofit your exemption prohibits you from limiting services to a particular individual or group. You are a helping organization and should not choose to limit services under any circumstances.

Line 3: You should check "No." You have a Conflict of Interest Policy, which prohibits this kind of behavior.

Part VII: Your History

Since you are a newly formed nonprofit and are submitting your 1023 Application promptly after incorporating, your answers to Lines 1 and 2 are "No."

<u>Lines 1 and 2:</u> Answer "No."

Part VIII: Your Specific Activities

<u>Line 1</u>: Answer "No."

<u>Line 2a:</u> Answer "No" and go to Line 3a.

<u>Line 2b:</u> Do not answer. Since you answered "No" to question 2a, no answer is required. Leave boxes blank.

<u>Lines 3a and 3b:</u> Check "No" for each question.

<u>Line 3c:</u> Do not answer. This question is not applicable to your nonprofit. Leave space blank.

<u>Lines 4a, 4b, and 4c:</u> Answer "No" for each question.

<u>Line 4d:</u> Write in "None."

<u>Line 4e:</u> Answer "No."

<u>Line 5:</u> Check "No."

<u>Line 6a:</u> Answer "No" and skip Line 6b.
<u>Lines 7a and 7b:</u> Answer "No" for each question and skip Line 7c.

Line 8: Answer "No."

Line 9a: Answer "No" and go to Line 10.

Lines 9b, 9c, and 9d: Do not answer. Skip these questions. They are not applicable to your nonprofit. Leave the boxes blank.

Line 10: Answer "No."

Line 11: Check "No."

Line 12a: Answer "No" and proceed to Line 13a.

Lines 12b, 12c, 12c, and 12d: Do not answer. Skip these questions. They are not applicable to your nonprofit. Leave the spaces blank.

Line 13a: Check "No" and go to Line 14a.

Lines 13b, 13c, 13d, 13e, and 13f: Do not answer. Skip these questions. They are not applicable to your nonprofit. Leave the boxes and space blank.

Line 14a: Answer "No" and move ahead to Line 15.

Lines 14b, 14c, 14d, 14e, and 14f: Do not answer. Skip these questions. They are not applicable to your nonprofit. Leave the boxes blank.

Lines 15, 16, 17, 18, 19, 20, 21, and 22: Answer "No" to each question.

Part IX: Financial Data

Statement of Revenues and Expenses

Lines 1 through 24: Use your Business Plan and Line Item Budget to assist you in completing this section with your anticipated revenues and expenses.

Since your nonprofit is new, your statement of revenues and expenses is your *projected* budget. As with your business plan, figure out what programs you are going to operate and what you will need to fund these programs. You might do well to seek help **if** you find this difficult or confusing. Take a deep breath.

Okay, look at what's required. Again, "if" you need help, ask a person experienced in accounting or filing 1023 Applications. Actually, the information asked for here is fairly simple and straightforward.   You merely need projected *revenues and expenses*. You're being asked, "Where will your money come from?" and "How will you spend this money?"

Balance Sheet (for your most recently completed tax year)

Lines 1through 18: Write in "0" for each line. Your nonprofit is just beginning. You have no whole dollar information to report since you have not filed a tax return as yet..

Line 19: Check the "No" box.

Part X: Public Charity Status

Line 1a: Check the "No" box and proceed to Line 5.

Lines 1b, 2, 3, and 4: Skip these questions and leave the boxes blank.

Lines 5a, 5b, 5c, 5d, 5e, and 5f: Leave these boxes blank as they do not pertain to your type of nonprofit.

Line 5g: Check this box as it describes your type of nonprofit.

Lines 5h and 5i: Leave these boxes blank.

Line 6a: Do not complete Line 6a. Request for Advance Ruling is not available.

Line 6b: Do not check the box. You are not requesting a definitive ruling.

Line 6b (i) (a): Per the instructions, "enter 2% of Line 8, Column (e) on Part IX-A Statement of Revenues and Expenses."

Line 6(i) (b): Check the box. All your financial data is projected, therefore the answer is "None."

Line 7: Check the "No" box.

Part XI User Fee Information

At the beginning of this chapter, you decided which fee you would pay based upon your anticipated average annual gross receipts over a four-year period. Keep in mind, too, that the fee for a 1023 on-line application may be less than the fee for a mailed-in application.

Line 1: If you anticipate your annual gross receipts will average *less than* $10,000 a year over a four-year period, check the "Yes" box and proceed to Line 2.

Line 1: If you anticipate your annual gross receipts will average *more than* $10,000 a year over a four-year period, check the "No" box and proceed to Line 3.

Line 2: Make out your $400.00 check or money order to the United States Treasury and check the box. Be sure include your payment in your mail-in 1023 Application package. If you are applying on-line, a $275.00 payment is required.

Line 3: Make out your $800.00 check or money order to the United States Treasury and check the box. Be sure include your payment in your mail-in 1023 Application package. The on-line payment is the same: $800.00.

Please Sign Here: Have an Officer, Director, Trustee, or other authorized official sign the 1023 form here. Type or print the signee's name and title or authority. Complete the date.

Schedules A through H

Schedules A, B, C, D, E, F, G, and H do not apply to your type of non-profit. Skip these schedules and leave them blank.

Form 1023 Checklist

Step 1: 1023 Application Fee Payment.

1. On your check or money order note your organization's name, EIN, and "1023 Application Fee."

2. Put your check or money order in an envelope.

3. DO NO STAPLE or attach, by any means, your check or money order to your application. Simply place it in the envelope.

4. Write your organization name, EIN, and "1023 Application Fee" on the envelope.

5. *When this step is complete, check the Second Box on the Form 1023 Checklist.*

Step 2: Application Completeness and Specific Details.

1. Review your application and be sure it is complete, including any requested information such as explanations and financial data. (None of Schedules A through H are required.)

2. Have you answered every question as instructed?

3. Are your purposes and proposed activities described in specific easily understood terms?

4. Have you provided *specific* details about your planned activities?

5. Does your financial information correspond with your proposed activities?

6. When you can answer yes to each of the above questions, your 1023 Application is ready for submission.

7. Generalizations or failure to answer questions will prevent your organization from receiving its 501 (c)(3) designation.

8. *When this step is complete, check the Fourth Box on the Form 1023 Checklist.*

Step 3: Include Exact Copy of Your Articles of Organization and Location of Purpose and Dissolution Clauses.

1. Do your Articles of Organization include the proper Purpose Clause? If yes, note the location--Page, Article, and Paragraph Number (from Part III, Line 1 on your 1023 Application)—on the Form 1023 Checklist.

2. Do your Articles of Organization include the proper Dissolution Clause? If yes, note the location--Page, Article, and Paragraph Number (from Part III, Line 2b or 2c on your 1023 Application)—on the Form 1023 Checklist

3. If your answer is no to either of the above questions, your 1023 Application is not complete and will not be approved for 501(c)(3) designation.

4. *When you have completed this step, check the Sixth Box on the Form 1023 Checklist.*

Step 4: Organization's Legal Name.

1. Is your organizations name on the application the same as your organizations' legal name as it appears in your articles of organization?

2. *If yes, check the Eighth Box on the Form 1023 Checklist.*

3. *If no, this needs to be corrected.* "Your organizations' name on the application must be the same as your legal name as it appears in your articles of organization." *Once this is corrected, check the Eighth Box on the Form 1023 Checklist.*

Step 5: Signature on 1023 Application.

1. *Has an officer, director, trustee, or other official who is authorized, signed Part XI of your 1023 Application?*

2. *If yes, check the Seventh Box on the Form 1023 Checklist. If no, have an authorized individual sign your application and check the Seventh Box on the Form 1023 Checklist.*

Step 6: Organization Name and EIN Labeling.

1. Label each page of every document with the name of your organization and EIN.

2. Make a copy of your EIN approval from the IRS to submit with your 1023 Application.

3. *When this step is complete, check the Third Box on the Form 1023 Checklist.*

Step 7: Schedules A through H.

1. You are submitting **no** schedules. Check the "No" box for every schedule listed.

2. *Then check the Fifth Box on the Form 1023 Checklist.*

Step 8: Assemble 1023 Application Documents.

1. Assemble your documents in this order from top to bottom:

   - Envelope with Check or Money Order
   - Form 1023 Checklist
   - Form 1023 Application.
   - Articles of Organization
   - Amendments to Articles of Organization in chronological order

48

- Bylaws
- All Other Attachments including EIN approval copy, explanations, financial data, and printed materials or publications.

2. When you have completed your package assembly, check the First Box on the Form 1023 Checklist.

Congratulations! Your 1023 Application Package is Complete!

Mail Your 1023 Application Package

If you are using regular mail, send your completed 1023 Application Package including payment to:

> Internal Revenue Service
> P.O. Box 192
> Covington, KY 41102-0192

If you are using express mail or a delivery service, such as FEDEX or UPS, send your completed 1023 Application Package including payment to:

> Internal Revenue Service
> 201 West Rivercenter Boulevard
> Attn: Extracting Stop 312
> Covington, KY 4011

6

BOARDS

Roberta was thinking out loud. "We need a board of directors. We need likeminded folks to help us handle out nonprofit's business and to help us to get that all important support."

"Yes, we need to have something permanent in place, run by folks who think like us, to help govern our nonprofit," Pooky chimed in.

They needed a board to be responsible for money, legal, and *tax matters.* Although the nonprofit will not have to pay taxes, it still needs to file a **financial report** to the IRS. Even if there is no financial information to report for the first year, the W990 still needs to be filed.

Since it governs the nonprofit, the board has many responsibilities:

1.   It comes up with the purpose, mission, and goals of the nonprofit.

2.   It does the planning for the nonprofit.

3.   The board chooses its chief executive.

4.   It sets up the policies and guidelines.

5.   The board hammers out and makes certain that there is a conflict of interest policy.
6.   It makes certain that there is fiscal soundness and is responsible for raising funds.

7.   It promotes good will. In effect, one of the main functions of the board will be to always serve as public relations spokespersons.

When putting your board together, you want to choose people who are **in complete agreement** with your nonprofit's purpose, mission, and goals.

Do not set up a board with people who you think will 'make your nonprofit look good'. Just having a *known* name on the board and on your stationary *is not* the approach to take. A 'so-called' known person on your board will not ensure that your nonprofit will be successful. Don't get me wrong. A person with a great reputation is really great for your board, if that person is **in complete agreement** with the purpose, mission and goals of your nonprofit.

On the other hand, it's just as important to leave a less reputable 'friend' off of your board. Reputations of board members count bigtime with those you want to support your efforts.

51

If you are just beginning, five strong people who are in complete agreement is a very good number to begin with. Make each one of those people count.

Pooky then asked Roberta an important question.

"If I'm on the board, am I going to be personally responsible for planning the programs, developing the programs, and putting them in action?"

"No ma'am, Ms. Pooky," said Roberta. "I've been asking, reading, and studying. It seems that the best way to get things accomplished is to have committees, instead of individuals, be responsible."

Roberta had an important point. The board could create or appoint committees to carry on the majority of the projects, programs, and other tasks. Committees could be one of the articles written into their bylaws. They could form the committees with the stipulation that a director from the board could head a committee. In fact, this would make one of the main responsibilities of the board, *to govern*, much easier.

"What kind of committees should we have?" Pooky wondered out loud.

"Well, I think that we should have committees that reflect how we are going to proceed with our programs and projects," Roberta answered.

Actually, Roberta had consulted a few people on a few boards and had decided that they could have both *standing and special committees.* The standing committees would be **permanent** committees.

Executive Committee, Planning Committee, Program Committee, Development Committee, and Financial Committee would be their *standing committees.* Each committee would be headed by a board member, who held those board positions.

The board or the board chairperson can, also, appoint or create *special committees* for special programs or projects.

"You did say that on e of the other responsibilities of the board is to help bring funds, right?' Asked Pooky. "What's the best way to do this?"

Roberta went on to explain that you had to make certain that everyone on the board realized that it was their responsibility to take part in bringing funds into the nonprofit. Each board member needs to be aware of how the entire board is going to go about raising funds by following the same plan and protocol.

It is important that each board member knows everything about their nonprofit. They cannot be effective fundraisers for an organization if they have not been made aware of the board's purpose and mission. As board members come aboard, they need to be made aware of the business plan.

One idea that helps create unity of purpose among your board members is to have the entire board participate in interactive fundraising workshops. These introduce them to fundraising ideas and approaches.

A good beginning for each board member is to commit to soliciting funds for the nonprofit. Each board member has friends and family that they can begin with. In a lot of cases, board members may be aware of others form the general public who can make large contributions. The important thing to remember is *to not be afraid* to ask friends, family or anyone that the board member feels can or will help. *Don't be afraid to ask.*

Then, the board has to have a fundraising plan. They need to first determine where funds are available for their specific programs and how the board or appropriate board committee will pursue these funds.

"Hey, this is falling into place," Pooky said. "In the 501(c)(3) application, we decided to check the box which stated that we'd get funds from the general public, from foundations, and from governmental entities."

"Right," answered Roberta. "I think that it'd be a grand idea to involve all of the standing committees, but to have the Financial and Development Committees head our fundraising plans and efforts. These committees can develop plans and programs which the planning and program committees have come up with. They will then know the amount of funds needed to successfully operate the programs."

7

COLLABORATION/PARTNERSHIPS

Whether you are just beginning your nonprofit, or it has been in existence for years, don't be afraid to collaborate with others in order to achieve the purpose and mission of your nonprofit.

All too often, because of competition for funding, 'turf battles,' and/or putting personal goals ahead of your organization's goals; many executive boards, directors, and members miss the opportunity to take advantage of having *collaborative partnerships.*

Take the attitude that working with someone else could greatly benefit your nonprofit. Find the collaborative partners that share your nonprofit's purpose and goals. Seriously consider working with them, then commit.

There are a lot of invaluable resources that other likeminded organizations, groups, institutions, and other entities have to offer. They may be able to provide needed program space, knowledge, information, people, or finances that will be helpful.

Who should your nonprofit choose to form collaborative partnerships with? For the vast majority of nonprofits, it has been found **that academia, other community groups, the business community, and governmental entities** are the most beneficial partners.

Academia

Teachers, Parent Teacher Organizations' or Associations' (PTO/PTA) members, schools, and educational professionals are dedicated to making improvements in the lives of others. They have something helpful to contribute to your nonprofit, *if you'll just ask*!

In a lot of instances, those associated with academia are working with age groups that you're working with. You might want to reach a group of students and have one of the most important groups in the school help you reach these students. There's no better grassroots education group than a PTO or PTA.

There's a possibility that your program may require a mentor for your music or art programs. A teacher as a collaborator is perfect.

Community colleges and universities can be valuable. They love to be a part of their communities. Ask them to use college or university space. These two entities will be glad to help. They're in the business of recruitment. They want potential students to be aware of their college or university. Those who are considered **academia** make wonderful collaborative partners.

Community Groups

Think about those who live in your community. Almost everyone in your community has something in common. It might simply be cultural. People, often, form community groups in order to achieve a goal or suit a purpose. For instance, there is the neighborhood association, the Everywoman's Flower Club, the church, the senior center whist club, the community athletic league.

There are scores of community groups that would be happy to help improve their community, *if they were just asked.* A community group is a great place to get a few volunteers for your nonprofit programs. **Community groups** and your nonprofit programs will usually share a common goal or purpose. You both want to improve or enhance members of the community.

The Business Community

Consider this. The **business community** is always anxious to help your nonprofit. It is good for their business!

You might have an assisted or assisted and supportive living facility for seniors. Your program needs transportation. *If you'll just ask* auto dealerships, you might find that they would be happy to help. It benefits them. All businesses strongly believe in advertising, promotion, and public relations. Those who manage businesses believe in a positive bottom line. They want to make a profit.

Being a good corporate neighbor is good for business. In this example, auto dealers know that positive publicity provided by them helping you transport senior citizens is going to help them eventually sell more cars.

One of your youth programs might be a mentoring program for a group of cheerleaders. They'll be cheerleading at community athletic events. Ask a community business to sponsor this group of cheerleaders by providing uniforms.

Each business that you approach will be interested if their participation will benefit their business. Credit given to them by the news story that your nonprofit provides will translate into eventual sales for them. Their business will be remembered. Everyone benefits.

Governmental Entities

A fourth important collaborative partner to your nonprofit is any governmental entity. It is vitally important that you are aware of the opportunity to collaborate with the many different parts of government at the city, county, regional, state, and federal levels. Take advantage of this opportunity. Local, state, and federal department continually solicit help from nonprofits and other organizations, because it benefits them.

Governmental entities like to work with other groups that can help them deliver their committed and/or obligated programs and services. You can help them keep their work. You and the entity both want to improve the lives of others.

START WITH THE DIFFERENT DEPARTMENTS AND THE FUNDS FOR PROGRAMS THAT ARE AVAILABLE.

The first thing that you want to do is familiarize yourself with your *local* forms of government. The form of government might be council, commission, metro, or some other form. You'll find one or two departments that are attempting to do exactly what you are doing, just on a much larger scale.

You might have a girl's volleyball program or a boys' softball team as one part of a youth program. See who is responsible for youth and recreation in your local government.

Your nonprofit might be involved with a program that trains participants in housing rehabilitation, construction, landscaping, or carpentry. Find out which local elected officials head these programs.

In the above two examples, you want to find out who or what department your nonprofit can benefit in fulfilling their local government initiatives and objectives. Believe it. They are looking for your nonprofit!

One of the most important government entities that will be a tremendous help to your nonprofit is your **public library**. Their mission is *helping*.

Over the past few months, public libraries have really demonstrated that a community is not just a location or place, but, most importantly, the people who live in the location. Libraries have realized and have made a successful attempt at being a vital part of communities. Libraries long to collaborate with organizations that improve people's quality of life.

In some instances, libraries often have available meeting space.

Libraries might be offering and teaching a cutting edge STEM (Science, Technology, Engineering, and Mathematics) Program or STEAM (Science, Technology, Engineering, Art, and Mathematics) Program.

Your nonprofit may have a tutoring or mentoring program that will benefit from programs and knowledge that you are not yet able to provide. Your nonprofit might feature a program that helps the unemployed apply for jobs or a program that assists with social security or disability help. *Ask your library* to collaborate with you regarding these programs. They have the technology and are, usually, staffed with persons who thrive on *helping*.

Forming Partnerships

Just how is your nonprofit going to go about developing these important collaborative partners from academia, other community groups, the business community, and governmental entities? Assign this task to one of your board committees. If you're just beginning and haven't created committees, then **you** will take the following approach.

Step One: Develop a Contact Database List.

Include the following information for each contact:

- Contact name, title, and decision making role
- Organization and department names
- Permanent location address and mail address
- Telephone numbers and email addresses

Step Two: Contact Decision Makers.

Write each contact a letter on your letterhead mentioning that you will follow-up with a phone call in a certain number of days.

Include a business card and any other information you might have.

If you don't have letterhead stationary, business cards, or brochures; do not let this stop you. It is the effort and information that is important. An 8-1/2" X 11" sheet of paper will do just fine.

Send out initial letters by regular mail. If they prefer to be contacted by email or other social media avenues, they will let you know.

Step Three: Telephone Follow-Up.

Follow-up with a phone call after the promised number of days mentioned in the letter.

During the phone call arrange a face-to-face meeting.

8

FUNDING

Every nonprofit organization, someone associated with a nonprofit, or everyone thinking about forming a nonprofit always asks the following "MONEY' questions:

1. How do I find funding?
2. Where can I find a grant?
3. How do I get a grant?
4. How long will it take before money comes?

Even before you begin looking for funding, decide what programs your nonprofit will be offering! Well thought out and effective programs always have the best chances of being funded!

The *first sources* that you should consider are *local* sources. If you have friends and acquaintances that believe in your purpose and programs, they are a great source of funds. This is a good place tyo begin. You will have some success. And once you have that first success, it will prove to you that you can indeed find funding from other sources.

Government Grants

Okay, you now want to know where your nonprofit can apply for governmental funding, specifically grants! The following is the *initial contact information* for departments where you will be able to find federal grants. If necessary, there is additional information available on the internet.

The Department of Health and Human Services (HHS).

This is a great place to search for grants for programs concerning the well-being of all Americans, especially youth, the elderly, and families.

Please go to HHS.gov. There is an entire section, which discusses grants and even has contact phone numbers. You will learn how to apply for grants.

If you feel that this is not working for you, find a person who writes grants. You can at least tell them where to look for the governmental department that has grant information for your transitional program for runaway teens, your daycare center, or your respite program for caregivers.

The Department of Education.

The department that issues grants for nonprofits that have an educational component as part of their overall program is The United States Department of Education.

Email address: ed.gov.

Mailing address: U.S. Department of Education
400 Maryland Avenue, S.W.
Washington, D.C. 20202

Your nonprofit might have a language teaching program that focuses on teaching American youth the Spanish language.

You want to provide GED training for high school dropouts.

You want to provide a diversity educational program at your childcare facility.

You want to collaborate with a local university as part of their discretionary grant program.

Your nonprofit might want to offer a program that educates the general public about the heritage and culture of a certain group of people.

Your nonprofit might want to teach quilting, chess, or archery.

If you feel that your nonprofit has a program that **educates**, you want to contact the U.S. Department of Education.

The Department of Housing and Urban Development (HUD)

Your nonprofit is looking for government grants that will help you provide certain programs and services for your assisted living facility. HUD is where you want to search. One helpful funding source is listed on the HUD website under **NOFA** (Notice of Funds Availability). Make us of this HUD NOFA site. If you want to see if this site has funding information that would benefit your program in any way, go immediately to this source. Again, you might need the help of an experienced grants person if you do not quite understand.

The United Stated Department of Justice (DOJ).

Your nonprofit wants to begin a preventative program for middle school youth. The program is designed to keep kids out of the juvenile justice court system. You just need funding to begin the first year. Your planning and development committees have plans in place to assure sustainability after the first year. The DOJ is a perfect place to search for funding.

The quickest way to become acquainted with the DOJ is through their website. You want to first go to their website www.justice.gov. The website contains all of the information that you will need to succeed. You'll find instructions on how to search for and submit grants. For your specific prevention program, you might first start at the Department of Justice Action Center. Also, be aware that since your program is a prevention program. You can also seek grant funding from the other previously named agencies. Look at your specific program and see if education, suitable housing, and the "well-being" programs that are offered by HHS are preventative programs.

Let's say that you want to offer an exciting new program for young ladies who are identified as "at risk." Your nonprofit has met with parents in your community. They have let you know that their kids have nothing that interests them beyond computers. Parents are worried that their girls are headed for the juvenile justice system, if someone or some organization in the community does not provide a new approach to the usual teen interests and problems. One father stated that he has actually heard his daughter talking to another young lady about starting a gang. He was aware that young ladies are now going to juvenile facilities at an alarming rate.

Okay, you decide that you want your nonprofit to offer a soft skills program for young ladies. Classes will be held in collaboration with local partners from a community college and the make-up department of a favorite local department store. There are potential funds for this program at **OJJDDP (Office of Juvenile Justice and Delinquency Prevention).**

It makes no difference where your community is located, youth face conflict and bullying from their peers. You want to offer an elementary school program which addresses these two major problems. You have designed a social media program that you know is going to really have kids participating. You are going to use their favorite tool and toy, the computer, exclusively for the program. Fortunately, there is Department of Justice funding for programs that address conflict, bullying, and anger management issues among our youth. You may have a conflict resolution program that will work with elementary school males and females. There are funding opportunities through OJJDP.

Foundation Grants

It's time that you become knowledgeable about **foundation grants**. There are hundreds of foundations that are important to your nonprofit if you're searching for organizations and other entities that distribute money for **charitable purposes**. I repeat there are hundreds. All you have to do is to spend the necessary time **researching**. You'll be surprised what you can accomplish if you'll just research.

By luck, years ago, I discovered a truly helpful source. I have to emphasize that I discovered this valuable source by luck! I was researching.

Before we get really deep into foundations and funding, reward yourself by using the internet to go to the following source:

Michigan State Libraries (Grants for Nonprofits)

A Michigan State Libraries WEBSITE will be displayed. Just look at all of the categories provided by this website. I guarantee that you'll find funding source information for your nonprofit program. Again, I discovered this source by luck, because I was researching.

You'll find all kinds of foundations ready, willing, and able to fund your programs. As I noted earlier, it benefits a foundation as much as it benefits your nonprofit for a foundation to provide funds for your program.

The first thing that you want to pay attention to is a foundation's *area of interest*. This is important. This information is contained in the foundation's website or RFP (Request for Proposal). Make certain that your area of interest matches the foundation's area of interest. Again, this is important. If your area of interest is to provide trucker training for trainees aged 18 to 35 years of age, you don't want to submit an application to a foundation whose area of interest is the aged.

Your nonprofit is establishing a program designed and dedicated to helping homeless and abused women to reconnect with their families. You're going to provide the basic food, shelter, and if necessary, clothing, for the enrollees in your program. You also want to provide a collaborative service with the business community, which will ensure the women employment while they are a part of your 6 to 12 month program. It's useless to apply to a funder whose only area of interest is in funding physical education programs for young women. You both have an area of interest in females, but different target age groups.

In another instance, you are rightfully aware that a certain well-known multimillion-dollar foundation has money for nonprofit corporations. Before you apply, make certain that this foundation has funding money to fund what your program is offering.

It's time for you to see how well you understand **areas of interest and RFP.** These are two terms that I previously mentioned.

First, go to *foundationcenter.org.*

Actually, my main purpose for directing you to this site is to introduce you to another terrific foundation funding source for your nonprofit. You're going to discover other grantors and funders, simply because you are researching the *foundationcenter.org* website.

It's possible that you have an exciting arts and culture idea that you want to begin in your community. *Foundationcenter.org* is where you want to begin researching! It's possible, that while you're on the *foundationcenter.org* website, you'll be lucky enough to be routed to the Grantsmakers in the Arts website. Take advantage and subscribe to this free website. It has loads of arts and culture grant funding information.

Please, take advantage of *foundationcenter.org*, a wonderful source of information regarding foundations that fund nonprofit organizations. If you don't see anything in your area of interest, click on *more proposals* and keep searching and researching.

I've introduced you to two major funding sites, the **Foundation Center** and **Michigan State Libraries**. Get to work. Practice exploring these two major sources. Once you discover how easily you are able to find these two sources, you'll realize that searching and researching is going to be very easy for you or your grants person.

Now you can begin a more detailed search for funding. First, go to any search engine such as dogpile, google, or safari, to name a few; and enter the program information for which you are want funding.

For example, you want to fund an at-risk youth program. Simply search for "foundations that fund nonprofit corporations serving at risk youth" or something along those lines.

If you're searching for community development or affordable housing grants for your program, follow the same procedure. Enter into a search engine something close to "foundation grants that fund nonprofits providing community development programs." You'll be happy to see that the following foundations may be able to help your program:

- Anheuser-Busch Foundation
- Bank of America Foundation
- Grammy Foundation
- Jones Family Foundation (Dallas Cowboys)
- Mazda Foundation
- Milagro Foundation
- Walmart Foundation
- Wells Fargo Foundation

These are just a few of the scores of foundations that fund at risk and/or community development programs. See if their area of interest matches your nonprofit's area of interest.

Volunteer to Raise Funds

Aramark offers nonprofits ways to make money to fund nonprofit programs. Approximately, seventy percent (70%) of nonprofits across the country are not familiar with Aramark partnership programs in a great many of our major sports teams and stadiums.

I became aware of this wonderful opportunity nine years ao at Turner Field, the Atlanta Braves Baseball Stadium. That summer, I discovered that Aramark was in charge of concession sales at the stadium. The provided a percentage of the sales to all nonprofits that would just become a part of their program. It gave the nonprofit that I was working with a chance to work and sell at 81 home baseball games. The nonprofit received ten percent (10%) of the sales. In addition to providing money for the nonprofit, the nonprofit was able to accomplish two other important things:

1. Members of the nonprofit had the opportunity to become closer by working together.

2. Because the nonprofit *had complete control over who it chose to work the games*, the nonprofit was able to provide summer jobs for members in the community.

To find out more about such opportunities in your community search online for Aramark's NPO Fundraising Programs. They have fundraising programs for nonprofits at sports stadiums across the country, including:

Soldier Field, Chicago   Quicken   Loans   Arena, Cleveland

Pepsi Center, Denver   Heinz Field, Pittsburgh

SAP Center, San Jose   Raymond   James Stadium, Tampa

The Verizon Center, Washington, D.C.

These are but a few of the stadiums where Aramark provides fundraising programs to help your nonprofit. It's up to your nonprofit to decide how much money you want to raise. Start your researching now.

Picture this. You're inside an arena or facility in Atlanta, Georgia, and your favorite entertainer is performing. Now, imagine your nonprofit in charge of one of the concession stations. Take the time to search and you may find that your nonprofit can help *fund itself.*

In entertainment venues across the country, Aramark provides a percentage of concession sales to nonprofits who take responsibility for manning the concession stations. Take advantage of this opportunity. Aramark is looking for a nonprofit like your nonprofit.

The NFL (National Football League) Foundation is another important source that you should research. The foundation *funds* and supports many diverse programs. Among these programs are youth literacy projects, obesity and wellness programs, breast cancer prevention and awareness initiatives, substance abuse programs, and medical care programs.

The National Football Foundation is not just about football. Your nonprofit can benefit from the foundation's community involvement if your purpose and mission is in keeping with this foundation's area of interest.

MLB (Major League Baseball) has teams and organizations that are eager to help nonprofit corporations. The Tampa Bay Rays, Seattle Mariners, The Atlanta Braves Foundation, and both The New York Mets and New York Yankees have a vested interest in helping their communities. These teams and organizations are looking to help a nonprofit that may be exactly like yours. Remember, your nonprofit corporation's programs will benefit Major League Baseball. Take advantage of the opportunity. Search and research.

Crowdfunding

You need to be aware of **crowdfunding** as a way to raise funds for your nonprofit. Crowdfunding gives you a way to raise money through the Internet from a large number of people who donate to your nonprofit. Since the late 1990's, single individuals, new start-up for-profit businesses, and entrepreneurs have been seriously taking advantage of crowdfunding as a way to fund projects and businesses.

An example of one hugely successful crowdfunding website is GoFundMe!

What is important is for you to see how simple it is to start a crowdfunding campaign. Pay attention to the process, because you're going to use this same process for your nonprofit organization.

Examine the **Official** GoFundMe website in detail. Learn everything you can about how a crowdfunding campaign is set up. What procedures are used? Follow the easy instructions to learn the process. You are not signing up with GoFundMe since it is primarily for individuals, for-profit businesses, and entrepreneurs. You want to learn the process, because you are going to use this same process for *your nonprofit organization.*

You are in luck. There are ***crowdfunding platforms for nonprofit corporations*** exactly like your nonprofit. Now you can utilize the process you learned studying the GoFundMe platform. Follow these three simple steps:

1.   Get online.

2.   Go to your favorite search engine. Dogpile, google, or safari are popular search engines.

3.   Type in "crowdfunding platforms for nonprofits."

You'll get a wealth of information.

You'll discover the crowdfunding platforms dedicated to nonprofits. You'll see the Top 10 and Top 11 sites as well as general information on crowdfunding for nonprofits and an introduction to crowdfunding.   Look closely at **Razoo, StartSomeGood, Crowdrise, and Kickstarter**.

As you examine different sites to see which ones may be best for your nonprofit, look for the answers to these questions:

- How long has the platform been in existence?
- Have there been any complaints of fraud?
- How does it generate traffic?
- What support will it offer your nonprofit?
- How will information be collected from your donors?
- What are its fees and how is payment made?
- What restrictions does it place on fundraising?
- How will your campaign be marketed?
- Does it allow for videos?
- How does it make use of Facebook, Twitter, and other social media to help you raise funds?

There is absolutely nothing to prevent your nonprofit from using this concept to raise money. Nonprofit crowdfunding platforms can help your nonprofit raise money and achieve your purpose. You can reach a large number of people throughout the world and introduce them to your nonprofit's new and exciting programs.

Do be keenly aware that at least 40 states and the District of Columbia *require that yo*u *register for fundraising* before you ask individuals to donate. It's a possibility that you will not have to register. Religious institutions and educational institutions are two organizations exempt from having to register for crowdfunding or any fundraising activities. However, be on the safe side. Contact the Department of Charities in your state.

Once you've done the necessary research to understand the crowdfunding process and the best platform for your organization, try it out. Remember, crowdfunding lets you reach out to the *world.*

Be sure to reach out to your nonprofit's world. Let everyone know about your crowdfunding efforts. To begin, create a database of contacts within your local community and community of interest. Include members of academia, heads of other community groups, individuals in the business community, and elected officials.

Send each contact in your database an invitation to contribute to your crowdfunding campaign. Be sure to include all the politicians. Don't be shy. They'll respond.

Send your message to every doctor, bank lender, insurance company agent, business executive, automobile dealership owner, and store owner you know. You'll be surprised at the response that you'll receive. The only thing that will keep potential funders from responding positively is that you don't make them aware of your nonprofit and its programs.

Fundraising Through Business Partnerships

There are numerous ways businesses can help your nonprofit with fundraising programs and donations. It's important that you research opportunities in your local community and on the Internet. I'm going to cover a few of these that are specifically designed to help your nonprofit.

Business Nonprofit Programs

Macy's Shop For A Cause. Twice a year Macy's offers a program to help your nonprofit. Search the Internet for details about how your nonprofit can participate in this program and contact them right away. They quickly respond and are very helpful. I have had only great experiences working with Macy's.

In a nutshell, Macy's give your nonprofit $5.00 coupons to sell. For every coupon sale made, your nonprofit keeps 100% of the money you collect. Purchasers of the coupons receive a $5.00 credit for each coupon and extra discounts on their purchases at Macy's during the promotion period.

Macy's provides everything you need to succeed, all the information and marketing tools. Then you decide how much money you want to make for your nonprofit.

Belk Charity Sale. Another department store that offers a similar promotion is Belk. Check with your local store or on the Internet for details.

Other Retailers in Your Area. Research online or visit local stores to inquire about promotional programs similar to Macy's and Belk or other programs they may have to assist local nonprofits such as yours.

Business Donations

Panera Bread's Day-End-Dough-Nation. If you are not aware of this program, search and find Panera's wonderful food program. I guarantee that it will benefit your nonprofit's purpose and those you serve. At the end of every day, Panera donates unsold products to nonprofits. This should peak your interest!

Starbucks' Make Your Mark Program. This is a "Matching Gift Program" that can help your nonprofit. Some Starbucks participate in this program. Some don't. There might be one in your community. How can you know? Search for it. Talk to the managers at your local Starbucks. You can't be certain, if you don't search.

Publix Community Program. In addition to a variety of diverse programs helpful to nonprofits. Publix has a program that mirrors the Panera Day-End-Dough-Nation program mentioned above.

<u>Corporate Contributions</u>. Donations from major companies can help fund your nonprofit programs. There are at least fifty-three (53) popular companies that donate to nonprofits.

These donations come in various forms. They may be available through annual giving, employee match grants, matched fundraising, or team volunteer grants.

Some of the well-known corporations that participate in one or more of these forms of donations are:

Bank of America	Chevron	Costco
Delta	General Electric	Google
Hilton Foundation	Kohl's	Kroger
Microsoft	Nike	Verizon
Whole Foods		

Again, all you have to do is spend time searching and researching. Talk with people. Use the Internet and the library. Ask librarians for help. They love to help. It's their job.

During your search, you'll probably discover smile.amazon.com (The Amazon Smile Foundation). Amazon will donate 0.5% of the purchase price of eligible AmazonSmile purchases to your nonprofit.

In-Kind Donations

Another type of donation that you need to know about is called *in-kind donation or in-kind contribution*. Often, you want to apply for a grant, but are discouraged or simply refuse to apply. Why? Because the grant calls for you to match funds that are offered in order for your nonprofit to be considered for funding.

Don't give up! See if you can provide *in-kind matching* rather than dollar-for-dollar matching. In-kind matching means that another person or entity can donate their time and/or service, and you can use this donated time and/or service as the needed matching funds for your grant application.

For example, you may be applying for a small grant of $10,000. One of the grant stipulations is that your nonprofit needs matching funds of $5,000 in order to apply. You have a corporate collaborative partner that, as a part of their community nonprofit programs, donates employee volunteer hours. This program can provide the matching funds you need.

Here's how it works. An individual or group of company employees agrees that they will donate 100 volunteer hours to your nonprofit during the grant-funding year. They value their time at $50.00 an hour. You now have your $5,000 dollars in matching funds and can apply for the grant.

What you'll need to include with your grant application is a letter that states:

1. That the in-kind donor agrees to allow the value of its donated service to be used for matching funds.

2. How much the donor values its in-kind volunteer work per hour.

3. That the donation will happen during the specific dates of the grant-funding period.

Remember this is just one example!

Promote Your Nonprofit with a Website

Donation Opportunity. Make certain that your nonprofit has a website. You can use your website to help with your fundraising efforts. Initially, people may visit your website just for information. Make certain that they have every opportunity to make a donation before they click off of your website.

Initial Experience. Your website needs to reflect what your nonprofit represents. If you consider your nonprofit to be "traditional," you want your website to reflect your "traditional values" with its content and appearance highlighting your traditional purpose and mission. You wouldn't want a website that's a little "offbeat" or "edgy."

Just as importantly, you wouldn't want a bland looking website if you want to attract those viewers and potential donors to the "cutting-edge programs" of your nonprofit. Let your website show what your nonprofit is about with what it looks like and what it says.

For example, you might have a nonprofit whose sole purpose is to help parents of "disabled" children have their child receive the same quality education and be treated the same as every student in their school. You wouldn't want a website that features images that have absolutely nothing to do with education or children.

First moments matter! Let your website represent and reflect you nonprofit in the very first seconds it is viewed.

Content. You want your website to have the basic information about your organization.

- State your mission and exactly what your nonprofit does, *in detail*.

- On your homepage, show something that highlights a successful program.

- Use a photograph or three.

- Make your information interesting.
- Make your potential donors want to know more about you.

- Let viewers (potential donors) know where you are located and all of your contact information.

- Introduce viewers to your wonderful reputable staff or an important collaborative partner.

All of the above can be done on your website.

Success Strategies

There are numerous ways to make your website attractive for any viewer, and especially attractive to potential donors. At the very least, try these five things to make your website compelling to donors.

1. Have your website designed to make a potential donor want to find out more about your nonprofit.

   - Do YOU personally like how it looks?
   - Do YOU personally want to find out more about your nonprofit and its programs?
   - What caught your attention? If it's not attracting YOUR attention, you can bet that it's not working.
   - Ask a few friends and strangers to comment on your website, even before launching it.

2. Have your website feature a weekly blog. Let the subject matter relate to things or ideas that are about your nonprofit's purpose.

   Your nonprofit might be focused on educating a specific age group of students. One week you might want to have an artist or an engineer discuss the STEAM (Science, Technology, Engineering, Art, and Mathematics) programs no popular across the United States. You might discover that readers are familiar with the STEM programs, but do not know that art has been added to this popular initiative.

   It's possible that you have a program whose sole focus is adults. Approach your local Social Security office and ask them to donate quarterly articles updating or mere discussing social security topics. Have someone from this office as your guest blogger.

3. Make it easy for people to sign-up or interact by email. It's a great way to develop a database.

4. Make your website fun. Take advantage of all social media streams available. Use videos and utilize color whenever possible.

5. *Above all else*, be certain that your website has a way for potential donors to donate.

9

NEED TO KNOW

To be successful, your nonprofit needs to be aware of many things it needs to do and vital information it needs to have. Some of this information may have been previously mentioned, but repetition is never bad. You'll find the majority of these ideas and this information helpful, and some absolutely essential to your nonprofit's success.

Articles of Incorporation (Charter)

It's *very important* that your nonprofit renews its Charter each year. This is especially important for 501(c)(3) tax-exempt corporations.

It's a widely held belief that once your Articles of Incorporation have fulfilled your 1023 Application requirement, that you no longer need your Charter. This is not true. There are times that your Articles of Incorporation might be a requirement, even though you have a designated 501(c)(3) status from the IRS.

You might need your Articles of Incorporation to open up the corporation's nonprofit bank account. You might apply for a local, state, or federal grant that calls for you to include your Articles of Incorporation.

Be sure to renew your Articles of Incorporation each year. You will usually be asked to do this by your Secretary of State every January. Typically, you have until April 1st to get this done. Renewal fees vary from state to state. The *average* renewal fee is $20.00 yearly.

The IRS Form 990

If you have a 501(c)(3), your nonprofit is required to file a Form 990 each year. This filing provides all information available to the public and confirms your nonprofit status. It, also, allows the IRS and other governmental agencies to be certain that you are not abusing your tax-exempt status.

You can file this by mailing in your Form 990 or completing a Form 990 online. It's a simple process. Among the questions that you'll be asked are to:

1. Identify your board members and their titles.
2. Identify any member who was paid over $100,000 in the year that you're filing. (Of course, you'll have no problem answering this.)
3. Identify your top three (3) programs, how they were funded, and your budget.

If your nonprofit's gross income is less than $200,000 for that year, you can file the short Form 990EZ.

If you do not file your Form 990 or 990EZ for three consecutive years, you have a major chance of losing your 501(c)(3) tax-exempt status. To avoid this, please file your Form 990 or 990EZ each and every year.

Required 501(c)(3) Five Year Report

When you receive your 501(c)(3) "Letter of Determination," if you asked for an advanced ruling from the IRS, this letter will inform you that you will have to report your status after five years. This allows the IRS to determine whether or not your nonprofit has abused its tax-exempt status. You **will not** be made aware of this reporting requirement again. Therefore, it's your responsibility to report your nonprofit status to the IRS. You will not get a letter reminding you of this obligation.

Nonprofit Insurance

It's paramount that your nonprofit has insurance. One of your budget's line items needs to be reserved for insurance. Your nonprofit can be covered in a variety of ways. I'd suggest that you look to nonprofit cooperatives first for insurance coverage. I'm suggesting this because it may be more economical for your particular nonprofit.

Do not forget the importance of research. If you're looking for an insurance company online, just place simple information into your favorite search engine. Something similar to "Insurance for Nonprofit Corporations" will get you started.

Try www.insurancefornonprofits.org if you're looking for a *cooperative group insurance company.* Group insurance is always cheaper.

Whichever company you choose, make certain that the company offers general liability, umbrella liability, *business* vehicle coverage, cove rage for leased vehicles, coverage for your directors and officers, and volunteer and/or participant coverage.

Nonprofit Bank Accounts

The following is needed to open a business account for your nonprofit:

1. A letter from your board of directors authorizing establishment of the account.
2. Your Articles of Incorporation
3. Your EIN
4. The name of your officers and their positions.
5. Some banks require a photo or social security number for each officer.

Your nonprofit has the same rights and privileges as a for-profit business. Definitely, do not be discouraged if you encounter a bank employee that is not familiar with establishing nonprofit accounts. Often, they just aren't trained on how to set up an account for a nonprofit. Be relentless until your account is established.

Okay, let's get to the usual question. You want to know if your nonprofit can borrow money. Yes, your nonprofit, certainly, can borrow money. Ask what the bank or lending institution's requirements are for loans. A majority of the time, collateral is needed. This is normal. Don't give up if you're just beginning your nonprofit. If you feel the need of a loan for your nonprofit, keep looking.

Request Help from Athletes

Have your nonprofit host a fundraiser that features a known athlete making an individual appearance at your fundraiser. Athletes are very open to projecting a good image. This, also, provides your nonprofit and the athlete with a fantastic photo op.

Most athletes have a foundation and/or manager. The first thing that you need to do is develop a list of three to five (3–5) athletes. After you've developed the list, make your approach through their manager or try their website for contact information.

The following is an actual example of how you can seize an opportunity. There is a nonprofit board director in Tampa, Florida, who is a barber. The quarterback of he Tampa Bay Buccaneers did a television photo op in the shop where the director works. He actually got his hair cut there.

The director jumped right on the opportunity and exchanged contact information with the quarterback's manager. He now is waiting on the Buccaneer's 2017-2018 football schedule to see when the Buccaneers have an off week. He'll then relay to the manager and quarterback the nonprofit's purpose and why it will be beneficial for the quarterback to make an appearance at the nonprofit's fundraiser.

Always, be prepared to take advantage of an opportunity.

Technical Assistance

You should <u>always</u> take advantage of grants the offer *technical assistance.* Simply because a grant offers technical assistance instead of funds does not mean that this is not the grant for your nonprofit.

You may feel that you do not have the expertise needed in certain vital areas. There are organizations across the country that offer *free* "technical help" for nonprofits, if you'll just take the time to contact these groups.

The United Way or United Fund in some cities offer technical assistance. Another great source is **Foundation Center**. Take the time to go into Foundation Center online to look for grants that offer technical assistance.

Get online and search for "organizations that offer technical assistance for nonprofit corporations." There are a variety of topics for which a majority of these organizations will help you develop or strengthen your skills. You might benefit from free help with topics ranging from strategic planning to collaboration, fundraising, forming boards, how to get the best from your board members, and teaching your nonprofit how to build on strengths that your nonprofit may already possess.

Demographics

Demographics are one of the necessities of any grant! Demographics identify the many important things that grantors look for when making a decision. Specific information that grantors look for is race, gender, poverty status, level of education, annual income, how many parents are in the home, what schools are in the community, and, often, what health care facilities are in your immediate community.

There are several online sites and ways to find the demographics that you need. For the majority of the sites, all you have to do is enter your zip code! The following sources are very good places to begin your search:

- United States Census Bureau (American Factfinder)
- City-Data.com
- National Center for Children In Poverty
- Movoto
- Your local Chamber of Commerce
- United States Department of Housing (HUD)
- The Huffington Post
- USDA.gov

No Political Activity

Again, I cannot emphasize too much how important it is that your nonprofit refrain from engaging in any and all political activity.

You probably feel that you can make a difference if you seriously involve yourself in politics. Well, you or other individual members or agents of your nonprofit certainly can. *But, your nonprofit cannot!*

This is extremely important to remember. Do not involve your brand new nonprofit or your 501(c)(3) tax-exempt corporation in any form of political activity. If you do, you will lose your tax-exempt status! Remember, you made a pledge not to involve your nonprofit either directly or indirectly in any political activity when you submitted your Form 1023 Application.

The IRS does not play. This means that your nonprofit cannot campaign, lobby, endorse, work on a telephone bank effort, or even put a sign in front of your registered office. If you do, you're violating your nonprofit Articles of Incorporation; and you're violating the IRS prohibition rule against involving your nonprofit in *any kind* of political activity. You will lose your nonprofit tax-exempt status.

The IRS even revoked the nonprofit tax-exempt status of The Association of the Bar of New York City for involving itself in political activity. The IRS does not play. Don't even "skirt the line" in having your nonprofit sponsor political debates or forums. Don't give any money to any candidate in the name of your nonprofit.

Until or unless things change, The Johnson Amendment is still in effect. You, personally, can do all of the aforementioned; but your nonprofit cannot.

Disclosures and Obligations

You need to understand that you have an obligation to disclose any requested information pertaining to your nonprofit. *Anyone from the general public* can ask to see information pertaining to your nonprofit. You are required to provide this information.

You might have it in your bylaws that the general public can see this information at your annual meeting, or you might want to make it available upon request. You can control this if you wish.

A donor or grantor may request to see any and all information regarding your nonprofit. Naturally, you'll have no problem doing this. Open disclosure is a requirement for all nonprofits. A potential funder even has the right to ask to see your original 1023 Application. You have nothing to hide. Provide a copy of that original application.

Just as importantly, when anyone makes a donation or contribution, give them a receipt. Give them the receipt at the time of the donation or contribution. This is a requirement. Make certain that you note *the fair market value if it's a contribution* other than dollars.

10

LETTERS

WRITE THOSE LETTERS

Sometimes, emails or contact by social media platforms will not accomplish what you want accomplished. There are many times that you will need to actually write letters, *especially, when you are making initial contact.*

You may need a letter to establish contact with a grantor, to reach an investor, to form a collaborative partnership, to offer an introduction to your nonprofit, or to send a simple thank you letter. Don't be tentative or shy. You can do this.

You will now be given examples of actual letters, which have been successful in achieving their purpose. Use them as a guide.

You can write a letter that will stir quick action. Pay attention
To all the necessary components needed for you to write a particular type of letter.

Example 1: Request Partnership with City Mayor

This first example concerns asking a ***mayor*** or a city to be a ***collaborative partner***. One of the most important things about communicating with certain elected officials is that you get their ***title*** and ***name*** correct. They are very serious about being addressed correctly. I'm serious. Your letter might not even be read, if the person feels as if they aren't given "due respect." After that, you want to include the usual who, what, when, and why.

Date

The Honorable _____
Address

Dear Mayor_____:

I am Your Name, Executive Director, of Your Nonprofit's Name, Inc. We are a newly designated 501(c)(3) ax exempt nonprofit corporation located in City, State.

We are in the process of establishing collaborative partnerships with governmental entities, the business community, academia, and other community groups in order to successfully realize our mission and purpose of improving the quality of life of residents of City, State.

Since viewing your appearance on the CBS Sunday Morning Show last Sunday, we know that you have a strong interest in heritage and preservation in our region of the country. Heritage and preservation is one of our major initiatives for FY 2017-2018. Our unique and aggressive approach developed by our board of directors is designed to guarantee many more visitors to our region. It will undoubtedly benefit your city, as many of the new visitors will want to visit historic City, State.

We would appreciate the opportunity to discuss how your involvement will benefit all involved. We realize that your time is valuable, but would like the opportunity to thoroughly discuss our programs with you and/or members of your staff.

During the next seven (7) to ten (10) days, the co-chairperson of our program committee will be contacting you to arrange a meeting to fully explain our programs and services. In the meantime, if you have any questions; please, feel free to contact me at <u>telephone number</u> or <u>email address.</u>

Sincerely,

<u>Your Signature</u>

Executive Director

Cc: Co-Chairperson Program Committee

Example 2: Request for Financial Support

This letter is another example and actual copy of an appeal for financial support sent out by an international nonprofit client.

The executive director created a form letter, which could be mailed to names on her database or used as a GoFundMe appeal. The usual W's (who, what, when, where, and why) are included in her letter. Then she adds another important W........*a website address.*

If your nonprofit does not have a web page, please get one. They're invaluable.

Date

Hi <u>Name of Contact from Database.</u>

Do you have a minute?

I'm, <u>Your Name,</u> Executive Director, of <u>Nonprofit's Name</u>, Inc. We are an international program located in <u>City, State.</u> Our nonprofit corporation is dedicated to greatly improving the lives of those who need special help, both in the United States and Africa. I'm working to engage people like you to support our 501(c)(3) nonprofit. We need your financial support now! Your support will help us complete and chart the future of our 2016-2017 missions.

An immediate 2016 need is help for our Sickle Cell Disease and Special Needs Advocacy Program. This program serves as the anchor to help Sickle Cell patients and to help support their families.

2017 will be a productive and beneficial year, with your help. We need funds for our 2017 "It Takes a Village" fundraising gala, which will be held at <u>Location Address</u> in <u>City, State.</u> Youth from Kenya will visit and perform at various locations along the East Coast of the United States. Our "Annual Broken Crayons Still Color Gala" fundraiser will be held in Atlanta, Georgia, during the summer. We need your support now! For the remainder of our 2017 programs, please take one more minute and visit our website at journeysbygrace.weebly.com

Sincerely,

<u>Signature</u>

Executive Director

Example 4: Request to Corporation for Help

Sometimes, there are "set aside" funds for nonprofits. This means that there are funds *set aside for a specific purpose.*

The following example is the actual and total letter to Macy's from a nonprofit in South Carolina. The name of the nonprofit is correct. You have to understand that in the Low Country of South Carolina they speak and spell a little differently.

Macy's responded with a yes, solved the logistics, and helped the nonprofit to be able to raise funds. The only thing needed was a *letter*, to solve a problem.

July 27, 2015

Ms. Sharon Kearney
Customer Service
Macy's
7804 Abercom
Savannah, GA 31406

Dear Ms. Kearney:

We are Embrella Visionz, a 501(c)(3) nonprofit corporation (47-3450968), located in Yemassee, SC.

We were recently approved by Macy's to participate in the August 29, 2015, Shop For A Cause fundraising event, with an initial 100 coupons. We have a problem, which, hopefully, you can help us solve. We were assigned to either the Columbia or Greenville, SC, stores. We are hours and miles away from both the Columbia and Greenville locations, but only fifty 50) miles from your Savannah location.

It would be beneficial for everyone, if we are able to partner with your Savannah location. Would a member of our program committee be able to pick up coupons and participate at your location?

We would appreciate any help and guidance that you can provide us in solving this problem.

Sincerely,

Roberta Patterson
Executive Director

Example 5: Request for Transportation Assistance

One of the major needs for a nonprofit is transportation. You may need a vehicle to deliver a social or medical service for senior citizen in your program. Your girls and guys sports teams might need transportation all year. You might need field trip transportation to the Tellus Science Museum, The Penn Center Museum and Gallery, National Jazz Museum, National Museum of African American History and Culture, Giant Sequoias and Museum.

A letter to a local auto dealership, or even a car rental agency that is changing year models, is worth your letter effort. Use the following *example* and write that letter.

Your Nonprofit's Name
Address

Date

Contact Person's Name, Title
            OR
Marketing or Community Relations Department
Dealership's Name
Address

Dear Contact Person's Name:

We are Your Nonprofit's Name, Inc., a 501(c)(3) corporation (include your 501(c)(3) number). We are in need of a (State what kind of vehicle that your nonprofit needs, and why you need it.).

In 2016, our program served over 700 participants, who are identified as "at risk" or underserved, in our community. During Funding Year 2017-2018, we have added additional programs, which will increase participation by 300+, over 2016. Your tax deductible contribution will add needed and increased mobility for our community residents.

We would appreciate your consideration of our request. The Co-Chairperson of our Development Committee will call you within ten day, and be prepared to answer your question at the time. If you have any question or need additional information before then, please contact me at
    telephone number or email.

Sincerely,

Your Signature

Your Name
Your Title

Cc: Co-Chairperson Development Committee

11

E P I L O G U E

It had been almost three months since they'd discussed their nonprofit plans. Roberta and Pooky stood in front of The Penn School on St. Helena Island. Penn School was the first school started down south for blacks after the Civil War. It provided the first formal education for Gullah Slaves freed after the Civil War.

Spring had been in the air on the Island for a few days. You could almost smell the Spanish moss that covers all of the ancient oak trees. The marsh grasses that are everywhere looked like they were getting ready to dance. It was seventy-two degrees, on this late day in February. Birds were chirping. Creatures were stirring. It might be a good day to go crabbing.

"Okay girl, right after Christmas, this is the date that we chose to make a decision about starting a nonprofit," Roberta said. "I think that in addition to the projects and programs that we discussed earlier, we have to preserve our Gullah history and culture above all else, Pooky. I know in my heart that our nonprofit is the last hope to do this. Our culture is either dying or being killed by commercial interests."

"Yeah, just look at what Walmart is doing on Lady's Island," Pooky chimed in. "Worse than that, I hear that the Beaufort Arts Council is shutting down, or being shut down."

"This probably means that the annual Gullah Festival that celebrates our history, our language, our food, and all of our customs is doomed," Roberta bemoaned.

"We should go ahead with our nonprofit plans," Pooky said in agreement."

"Okay, let's start our nonprofit. Let's begin no later that March 15th. This is going to be our beginning date to save a lot of things and help a lot of people here in the Low Country. Roberta, do you think that your friend will help us to understand how to do what we want to do?"

"I'm certain. During the Christmas holidays, I looked at parts of the book that he was writing. He even let me help edit a few pages of the funding chapter. We need the book. Even *you* can understand THIS book, Pooky. It's easy reading." Roberta said laughing.

"Seriously, from what I read during Christmas, everything that we need to know about how to start our new nonprofit will be in this book. It tells how to go about getting that 501(c)(3) that we need."

"The book explains tax exempt status, and how it will help us. I got a great idea of how our tax exempt status helps us and whoever might be funding our nonprofit programs. This exempt status seriously benefits a business or foundation, and even a person making a donation; because they can take a tax deduction."

Pooky was now listening closely. She knew how Roberta was once she started talking.

"One of the most important chapters that I saw was the chapter on a business plan. The chapter just didn't talk about how our nonprofit will need a business plan, but explained *step-by-step* on how to go about writing a business plan! "

"I couldn't get over how this step-by-step business plan approach helped me understand what we need to do. The plan discussed strategy, marketing, service issues, financial issues, how to create a budget, how to figure out our strengths, how to see if we have any weaknesses, identifying and taking advantage of the opportunities that we have to help, and what threats are usually out there for a new nonprofit or any business."

"Actually, the only real threat that I see is us. If we are, or get lazy, we can't and won't succeed." Roberta was on a roll now.

"I had to check myself, when I went over a few points in the Partnerships/Collaboration Chapter. I know that probably in past situations, I might have been slow about wanting to work with another person or group. But, if we seriously want to have our programs make an impact, it's important that we work with others, Pooky. We have to take the lead in pointing out that "more heads are better than one." This chapter in the book really made me look at myself and promise myself that I would collaborate and partner with other groups right here in the Low Country to help the folks that we say that we want to help."

Pooky cut in, "Okay, Ro, we need money to do what we plan to do. How do we go about finding money, honey?"

"Like I said before, Pooky, I did get a chance to look at a few pages of the funding chapter. It discusses funding in detail. However, I came to realize that if we first get our programs, projects, and services together; we won't have to worry about finding money. Programs are what are important. Programs beget money, honey!! Foundations, businesses, and even governmental entities are just looking for nonprofits that have meaningful, beneficial programs."

Pooky could tell that Roberta was excited.

"I was promised that I'd get the very first autographed copy of this book, as soon as it's copyrighted and printed." Roberta was still talking faster now. "There's so much valuable information in the parts that I did get to see. I know that the rest of the book is just as valuable."

Pooky was thinking out loud. "Okay, I'm sold."

"We can talk some more after we get back from crabbing. I know that you have some raw chicken necks to use for bait in out pots. Uh…leave the chicken feet at home."

They both just laughed and laughed.

Made in the USA
Columbia, SC
26 April 2025